A CAMBRIDGE TOPIC BOOK

Life in the Iron Age

Peter J. Reynolds

Published in cooperation with Cambridge University Press
Lerner Publications Company, Minneapolis

Editors' Note: In preparing this edition of *The Cambridge Topic Books* for publication, the editors have made only a few minor changes in the original material. In some isolated cases, British spelling and usage were altered in order to avoid possible confusion for our readers. Whenever necessary, information was added to clarify references to people, places, and events in British history. An index was also provided in each volume.

LIBRARY OF CONGRESS CATALOGING IN PUBLICATION DATA

Reynolds, Peter John
Life in the iron age.

(A Cambridge Topic Book)
Originally published under title: Farming in the iron age.
Includes index.
SUMMARY: An account of farming, building, and daily life during the Iron Age in Britain based on experimental archaeological reconstructions.
1. Iron age—Great Britain—Juvenile literature. 2. Agriculture—History—Juvenile literature. 3. Great Britain—Antiquities—Juvenile literature. 4. Farm life—Great Britain—History—Juvenile literature. [1. Iron Age. 2. Agriculture—History. 3. Great Britain—Antiquities] I. Title.

GN780.22.G7R49 1979   631'.09362   78-56800
ISBN 0-8225-1214-9

This edition first published 1979 by Lerner Publications Company
by permission of Cambridge University Press.

International Standard Book Number: 0-8225-1214-9
Library of Congress Catalog Card Number: 78-56800

Manufactured in the United States of America

This edition is available exclusively from:
Lerner Publications Company, 241 First Avenue North, Minneapolis, Minnesota 55401

Contents

INTRODUCTION

In Britain, the period of time known as the Iron Age spans roughly the seven hundred years before the birth of Christ. It is called the Iron Age because it was during this time that iron was used to manufacture tools and weapons for the first time. This does not mean that the metal was very common. Iron, of course, rusts away fairly quickly, so that we cannot be sure how common it really was. Comparatively few iron objects have survived and most of those that have are very corroded indeed. Another reason for calling it the Iron Age rather than anything else is that we have no written records except for the occasional comment by a Greek or Roman writer.

How do we know about the Iron Age?

Our evidence for the Iron Age comes mainly from excavations carried out by archaeologists during the last fifty years or so. It is from the results of such excavations that we try to reconstruct and understand the houses, structures, defences, weapons and tools of the Iron Age period and the processes that all these things involved. In fact we have to adopt the role of the detective who has to use all the evidence available to reconstruct the 'crime'. Because the events we are interested in happened over two thousand years ago, our job is much more difficult. Just as the detective can make mistakes, be misled by false clues and weak evidence, so can we make enormous mistakes. Especially is this true because the quantity of our evidence is so small and often the quality is very poor as well. Unlike the detective who can ask questions of people, we can only ask questions of holes in the ground, ditches and banks, fragments of pottery, broken tools and similar objects. In fact we are trying to reconstruct the way people lived by examining the rubbish that has been left behind. This means using that misleading kind of information called circumstantial evidence.

Two other types of evidence can also be used. Sometimes the comments of Greek and Roman writers are helpful, especially when they are simply giving a description rather than making a political point. Often it is possible to match their words with the archaeological remains. This immediately strengthens the evidence. The second type of evidence we can use is that of modern observation. In certain places in the world we believe we can see an Iron Age way of life still going on today because in such places the people are creating the same kind of archaeological evidence that has been recovered from excavations. Again we must be especially careful of this comparative kind of evidence and use it as a guide rather than an answer. Because many of these 'modern Iron Age' societies live in remote areas, we have to consider all the varying factors and test them properly. Perhaps the most important difference we need to consider is the climate. We believe the weather in the Iron Age period was not very different from the weather today. Therefore to learn about Iron Age Britain we can only compare the modern places that have the same kind of weather as Britain has. An Iron Age house, for example, may look rather like an African house but its construction must be stronger and, therefore, different.

Archaeologists studying the Iron Age in Britain can also make use of information supplied by a unique research project being conducted at the Butser Ancient Farm in Hampshire, England. At the Butser Farm, an Iron Age farmstead has been reconstructed, and archaeological theories about Iron Age agriculture are being tested by controlled experiments. Many of these exciting experiments are described and pictured in this book.

In working with these different kinds of evidence, we must be sure to use common sense and logic, just as a detective does. We must avoid jumping to conclusions. Perhaps the story of Iron Age farming as told in this book is almost right, perhaps it is largely wrong. As more excavations take place and more evidence is discovered we shall need to revise the story in places. In ten years' time we may even have to rewrite the whole story. Meanwhile the case must always be kept open . . .

This photograph shows the Iron Age farmstead at the Butser Ancient Farm Research Project in Hampshire, England. You can see in the foreground sheep pens with hurdle fences around them, the first two roundhouses of the farmstead and, beyond, the field system upon which ancient types of grain are being grown. On the right, beyond the sheep pens, are two haystacks, one with a conical thatched roof. The woods in the area provide timber for building and fencing. In the distance is the valley of the Mean river.

1 SPRING

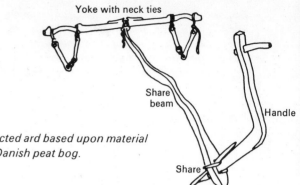

A reconstructed ard based upon material found in a Danish peat bog.

Some things about farming have not changed much since the time of the first farmers thousands of years ago. The ground has to be prepared for the seed; the seed has to be planted and tended during the growing period; the crop must be reaped at harvest time and stored carefully until it is needed either for preparation as food or to be sown as seed again the following season. Animals have to be looked after, fed and watered. They must have special care at calving and lambing times. Farmers have to trade, selling their products, buying new stock and supplies. The agricultural cycle does not really change. What is different from age to age is the way in which all these activities are done.

Modern farmers scarcely know how farmers of a hundred years ago managed their land. Without all the complex machines like tractors, harvesters and grain driers many farmers today would not know how to begin. An even greater difference lies in the widespread use of chemicals to do the tasks once done by people themselves. Yet all these are relatively modern inventions.

So in tackling the problem of understanding how farmers worked in the Iron Age, over two thousand years ago, we begin with the basic facts that plants grow according to the seasons, and that in order to get the best out of those plants certain processes have to take place. To find out more we must use the different kinds of evidence described on page 4.

Plowing

Plows

What happened in the spring time? How did the Iron Age farmers break up the ground? What sort of plows did they have and what sort of animals pulled them? Although there is extremely little evidence for actual plows in Britain, we are very lucky because several plows have been found preserved by tannic acid in the peat bogs of Denmark. In fact these are not real plows at all. They are called ards because they do not

possess a moldboard which turns the soil over. The ard is simply a spike which digs a furrow in the ground. On some excavations in Britain, marks made in the subsoil by such an implement have been noticed by archaeologists. The marks are frequently in a criss-cross pattern suggesting that the ground was plowed in two directions in order to stir up the soil thoroughly. Several experiments have been made using copies of the prehistoric ard to see how efficient they can be. Quite deep furrows were produced.

We can imagine, therefore, that as soon as the cold, wet weather began to give way to the drying winds of March, the farmers took out the plows they had repaired, or even made, during the short dark days of winter and checked the joints and fastenings. Then the farmers lifted down the yokes from the roofs of the roundhouses where they had hung being seasoned by the smoke from the hearth, tested the twisted halters for strength and finally prepared their ox teams for work.

The plow team

The sort of cattle that were alive in the Iron Age no longer exist. By studying the bones dug up by archaeologists, scientists are able to tell how big and heavy the beasts were. The Latin name given to the Iron Age cattle is *bos longifrons*. The nearest modern parallel to these cattle is a cross between the very small Dexter cow and the Kerry cow. The picture on the opposite page shows two animals which are just about the actual size and shape of the original *bos longifrons*. These particular animals are being trained to pull an ard in order to carry out more experiments in prehistoric plowing.

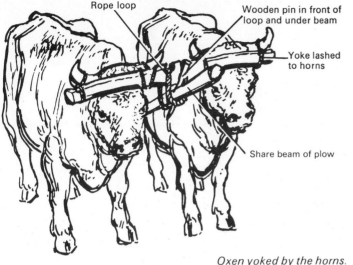

Rope loop

Wooden pin in front of loop and under beam

Yoke lashed to horns

Share beam of plow

Oxen yoked by the horns.

The dark lines show the angle of pull when oxen are yoked by the horns (above)*, and by the neck* (below)*.*

Oxen yoked by the neck.

Yokes

After the winter the farmers would have to spend some time preparing the oxen to work again, getting them used to the yoke about their necks and the weight of the plow biting into the ground behind them. It is probable that the farmers would have one older animal yoked to a younger one so that they would always have one trained animal to show the other how to work. This is the normal practice in some parts of Spain where oxen are still used to pull ards.

Exactly how the ard was attached to the yoke and the yoke to the oxen we do not know. Again we can look to countries where they are still used to find a possible answer, but even here there is difficulty. In some cases the yoke is fixed to the horns of the oxen; in others it is attached to their necks. Which system is best is often the cause of heated argument between neighbouring farmers. With the yoke fixed to the horns of the oxen the best line of pull is obtained. The diagram shows that the angle of the beam of the bog ards makes it seem likely that the yoke was fixed to the horns. The advantage of the neck yoke, on the other hand, is that the ox is free to move its head from side to side. No doubt the argument raged just as fiercely in the Iron Age.

Aerial photograph of Celtic fields on Smacam Down in Dorset. You can see how the lynchets have formed on the sloping ground.

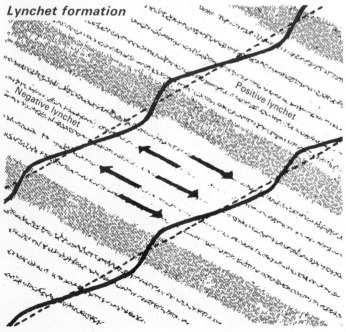

Lynchet formation

Negative lynchet

Positive lynchet

Fields and lynchets

The farmers would have already decided which fields to plow and which to leave fallow, and would set off with the ards over their shoulders, leading the oxen to their work. We have a rough idea of the size of the fields because in many parts of Britain, especially on the high chalky land in the south, we can see the remains of farming activities on the hillsides. Because farmers sometimes plowed fields on sloping ground, small banks grew on the downhill boundary. These banks are called lynchets, and were formed by the steady, slow movement of the soil downhill. In some places these lynchets are 2 or more metres (2-3 yards) high. The lynchets show the area of some of the fields. A general estimate of their size is 0.2 of a hectare (½ acre) or in farming terms, the amount one person and an ox team can plow in one day. In countries where this type of agriculture is carried on today, fields of a similar size are to be seen.

left: *The dotted line shows the original slope. The arrows indicate the directions of plowing along the contours.*

Harrowing

Once the land has been plowed, the farmers have still to make it into a good seed-bed. It is no good sowing the seed straight into deep furrows because much of it would be too deep to grow properly. Another operation has to take place before planting. Perhaps the oxen were used again, this time dragging a beam or heavy wooden board across the furrows to level them out and break down still further the clods of earth. Perhaps we shall never know for certain, though it is possible that some heavy pear-shaped stones which show signs of wear at one end may offer a clue. Perhaps these stones were wedged into a wicker hurdle by the narrow end while the more bulbous part projected underneath. The wear could be caused by their being dragged across the ground. Such a device is sometimes used in threshing grain, and it could well have had a double purpose.

The seed

Sowing

The methods of planting the seed again present enormous difficulties. Did the farmers scatter the seed over the top of the ground, as the Romans did? The answer is probably no. The Iron Age farmers, unlike the Romans, did not possess harrows to cover up the scattered seed and draw it into lines. It is much more likely that they made shallow furrows with a curved stick, or else planted in individual seed holes. Certainly sowing was a time which involved all the people of the farmstead. Every available person would be hard at work to get the seed planted as quickly as possible. The scene would be little different from the sight of potato pickers at work today — fields full of bending figures intent on getting the job completed.

far left: *Drawing a shallow furrow.*

left: *Using a stick to poke holes for seeds.*

bottom left: *Putting the seed into the holes.*

above: *Grain impressions of barley on the base of a beaker from North Berwick, Scotland.*

left: *Grauballe Man. A body preserved in a peat bog in Denmark, discovered in 1952. The body was probably cast into the bog about A.D. 300. His throat had been slit.*

Types of seed

What sort of seed did they plant? Here we have much more certain knowledge. On many excavations carbonized seeds have been discovered. Carbonized seeds are seeds which have been exposed to considerable heat and have been turned into carbon rather than burnt away (like a cake which has been left in the oven too long). Indeed this is quite possibly what had happened to the carbonized seed that has been found. By carefully studying these remains botanists are able to identify exactly what kind of seed it is. Another form of evidence that is quite common is seed impressions fired into pottery. Just as dog paw prints are found on Roman roofing tiles (caused by a dog running across the tiles as they are laid out to dry on the ground), so the Iron Age potter has been careless in the drying of his pots. He has let them lie on the ground and pick up seeds

on the soft clay surface. Then during the firing process the seed has been burned away but the impression remains for ever, to be discovered by the archaeologist.

One other way of discovering the seeds cultivated or collected by Iron Age man, much more dramatic than either the pottery impressions or the carbonized seed, has been the discovery of bodies in the Danish bogs. As it has preserved wooden objects, the tannic acid has also preserved the flesh of these men for thousands of years. Exactly why the bodies are to be found in the bogs is still not certain. One idea is that they were criminals who were first strangled and then thrown into the bog. Another is that they were 'sacrificed' as victims in a religious ceremony. Whatever the reason may be, because the bodies have been so well preserved, so have the contents of their stomachs. Scientists have been able to examine the bog men's last meal and to tell us what they had eaten. We cannot be sure that their last meal was what they usually ate because, since they may have been condemned men they may have had to eat a special meal. But even as a special meal it does represent some of the things that were eaten then.

Varieties of crop

By using all the pieces of evidence so far discovered, we know that by about 300 B.C. the Iron Age farmer grew certain types of wheat, barley and oats (see the drawings on page 37).

The wheats of the Iron Age, usually emmer and spelt, are still grown in more remote parts of the world. One particular feature of these early wheats, especially emmer, is the long beard or awn on the florets which contain the grain.

The cereal most often grown in the later Iron Age seems to have been barley. The early forms of barley are much more like the modern varieties, and much easier to thresh than emmer or spelt. (There is more about reaping and threshing on page 38.) Although barley was normally used for food, there was another purpose. This was the brewing of beer, a popular tradition which has lasted right up to today. How beer may have been discovered is explained at the end of chapter 5.

The farmer also grew vegetables, vetch and especially a small field bean called Celtic beans. These are similar to modern field beans but of much smaller size, halfway between a pea and a modern bean. We suspect that a plant called 'fat hen' which we now think of as a weed was also used as a vegetable then. It has since been replaced by cabbage and spinach but it has a richer food value than either of them. (There is a drawing of this plant on page 40.)

Crop rotation

In trying to understand how the farmer used his land, the knowledge that beans were grown is very important. Wheat and barley, in fact all the cereals, use up nitrogen from the ground as they grow. Therefore, unless the farmer rests the fields and leaves them fallow, the ground becomes exhausted and useless. But the bean puts nitrogen back into the ground as it grows. So by careful planning and rotating the crops a farmer can use all his fields all the time by first growing two years of cereals, followed by one year of beans and then cereals again. In this way the land need never lie idle. But we can never be sure about

whether this was done in Iron Age farming. The farmer may have grown the same crop on the same fields repeatedly. Modern research suggests that this is quite possible and there is no need to rotate crops.

Manure

One other piece of archaeological detective work has suggested another important practice. On some fields which have been excavated, broken pieces of pottery, called sherds, have been found but no trace at all of houses or buildings of any kind. How did the pottery get there? Far too many sherds are present to be explained away by the labourers breaking the odd pot of beer. One way the sherds could have arrived on the fields was if manure from the farmstead were spread on to the fields. Since the manure heap was probably then, as now, the place where all the household refuse is thrown, a large quantity of sherds there would not be surprising. Imagine how much crockery is broken in the home over a year and thrown away. If the theory is correct, and it seems the best answer at the moment, the farmer also manured his fields, putting goodness back into the ground every year. This could be yet another indication that he did not let the ground lie idle.

Weeding

Once the farmer had planted the seed his tasks had only just begun. Today the farmers rely on chemical sprays to kill off the weeds and pests which damage the growing crops. Then it was a matter of careful and regular hoeing to keep the fields clear of the choking weeds until the growing plants were tall enough and strong enough to survive. Not only did weeds present a terrible threat but also the birds were a constant nuisance. Perhaps the children of the farmstead had to make sure that the birds were kept off the fields. By keeping careful watch and frightening the birds away they would be doing their share of the work. We can be sure that every member of the farmstead from the youngest to the oldest was involved in the farmwork in some way.

Almost as soon as the planting season was over the farmer was faced with calving and lambing time. This part of the spring work needs a special chapter.

2 THE FARM ANIMALS

What kind of animals did the Iron Age farmers have on their farm?

Cattle

We have already seen that they kept oxen to pull their plows. There is no real evidence about how they looked after them, but it is certain that oxen were special animals and received special care. Perhaps they even lived inside the farmhouse in an area separated from the living area by a simple partition. Because we believe that manure was collected and spread on the fields in the spring, the cattle must have been penned up somewhere for the winter, if only to make the manure.

There is another reason which supports the idea of cattle being kept in the farmstead all the year round. We know that a cow or ox will not eat anything that it has stepped on or dropped manure upon. It is much more sensible, therefore, to bring grass to the cow rather than let it wander freely in the fields. It is common practice to do this in some remote parts of Europe today, and a very modern system called 'zero-grazing' has been recently 'invented' which is based on the same principle. The cattle are kept in a barn and grass is cut by machine and brought to them. The Iron Age farmers would have found that their small fields could provide more food if they collected it themselves. Also, animals kept in the farmhouse would be much more domesticated than modern ones, important when they were needed to work as well as provide milk and meat.

Sheep

Sheep, on the other hand, cannot be kept in this way at all. They need to pull at the grass and generally will not eat grass that has been already cut down. It is fortunate that in Britain the prehistoric type of sheep has survived the last two thousand years on the remote St Kilda Islands off the north-west coast of Scotland. This breed is called Soay. We know they are the same animals because when sheep bones dug up by archaeologists are compared with the Soay sheep skeleton, they are exactly the same. But these sheep have survived in the wild state, and in order to study them closely we have first to redomesticate them. The Soay sheep is quite small. It looks very similar to a goat and it is difficult sometimes to distinguish the difference between sheep and goat bones. Because it is so small there is little meat on the carcass. Therefore we believe that it was kept particularly for its wool which would have been spun into yarn and woven into cloth on a loom. (This process is described on pages 45 and 46.)

left: *A Dexter cow with unusually long legs, similar to the extinct prehistoric cow* (bos longifrons). *This type of cow was bred from the Kerry cattle in Ireland.*

Soay ewe with a four-hour-old lamb.

and woven into cloth on a loom. (This process is described on pages 45 and 46.)

Lambing time is much later than with modern sheep, taking place in late April and early May. This would be an anxious time for the farmer because he would want to maintain a good flock in order to have enough wool for clothing. In northern Scotland where memories of keeping Soay sheep still survive, it is said that a flock of twenty mature Soay sheep will clothe a family of five people for a year. This gives a rough idea of the size of flock to number of people but it is not really reliable evidence for the Iron Age.

The wool is taken from the Soay sheep in late May or early June, a few weeks after lambing. The process is not the same as the modern way of shearing sheep. The wool is plucked or rolled off the animal. If this is not done the sheep rub it off on trees and bushes. The modern sheep, if it is not sheared, will almost suffocate in the hot days of summer. This shows the influence man has had on the animals he has domesticated. After a long period of time the animal becomes dependent upon man's care and attention. The Soay sheep is much nearer to being a wild animal.

Another possible use for the Soay sheep is the provision of milk, especially during the early summer.

Exmoor pony and foal.

Goats

The other animals of an Iron Age farmstead are a little more difficult to identify. Certainly there were goats but we do not really know the exact type. These would have provided milk, meat and hair as well as leather. Goat skin has been traditionally used to make containers for liquids. Descriptions of the old English goat could easily be mistaken for descriptions of the Soay sheep.

Horses

Horses were also important in the Iron Age and could well have been used as draft animals. The nearest modern relative of the Iron Age horse is the Exmoor pony, a strong and extremely hardy beast. Caesar describes how when he invaded their country in 55 B.C. the Britons used horse-drawn chariots with incredible skill. Perhaps they also used them to draw the ard, carts and other vehicles. We can be certain that every animal

left: *A horse on a late Iron Age coin (first century A.D.) of the Dobunnic tribe in the west of England. (Almost twice actual size.)*

right: *A skull of a prehistoric horse excavated from an Iron Age site in Hampshire. (Scale in inches.)*

below: *The White Horse of Uffington, Berkshire. This design was cut into the chalk rock, probably in the Iron Age. It can be seen from many miles away.*

had an important part to play in the economy of the farmstead.

One major problem concerning the Iron Age horse is the lack of horse bones from excavations. Occasionally several are found on one site. The picture shows a horse skull discovered in a pit inside an Iron Age enclosure. Perhaps we should think of the horse as a special animal which received special treatment. From Caesar's writings we know it was used in warfare, and in the later Iron Age it appears on the reverse side of some coins. Indeed some of the horse representations on the coins are magnificent designs, almost in the style of abstract art. Also throughout the Iron Age horse trappings, like mouth bits and bridle ornaments, have been found. Add to these pieces of evidence the lack of horse bones from excavations, and we might propose a theory that when horses died or were killed they received special treatment. In Europe they were sometimes buried in ceremonial chariot burials, but in England very little evidence for this kind of treatment has been found.

A detail of a panel of the Gundestrup Cauldron which shows a Celtic god holding in his hands men bearing aloft wild boars. It is difficult to decide what the other animals are. (Probably made in the first century B.C.).

Pigs

Pigs were definitely kept by Iron Age farmers and representations of pigs often appear on special objects. A famous silver bowl called the Gundestrup Cauldron was found in Denmark and the pig or boar is beautifully represented on it. Bones of pigs are often found in excavations. But how they were kept is very difficult to determine.

Although the European wild boar is a direct descendant of the prehistoric pig it is a very fierce animal indeed and hardly fits into the domestic organization of a farmstead. So far we have not really found any clear evidence of pig sties although some arrangements of post-holes might be explained in this way. In fact the pig may have existed in two distinct states: first the wild pig which was hunted for food and sport, and second the domestic pig which was kept for meat. Perhaps the wild pig is the one represented on art objects. Certainly there is a long written tradition throughout Europe of boar hunting, begin-

ning as long ago as Homeric times. Perhaps in time and when enough bones have been found, the zoologists will be able to tell us the differences between the bones of domestic pigs and wild pigs. Then we may be able to work out more about which types were kept. Recently an experiment at the Butser Ancient Farm was carried out which mated the European wild boar with a Tamworth sow, the oldest extant variety of pig in England. The piglets were remarkable for the brown and yellow stripes, but they proved to be more like the boar than the sow.

To farmers the pig can be a very useful animal beyond simply providing regular supplies of meat. By nature the pigs root up the soil in their search for food and, if they are kept in a field, in a very short time they tear up the grass and stir up the ground just as a plow does. At the same time they fertilize the land. It is possible that the farmers would have used the pigs instead of a plow, and then planted their cereal crops directly into the ground. An area pigs have dug up is called a 'pannage'. More work needs to be done by the archaeologists and

researchers to test this theory. They could first excavate the pannage to see what it looks like. They could then compare the result with excavations of Iron Age fields to see if there are similarities. Planting into pannage is definitely less work than plowing a field.

above left: *A wild boar* (sus scrofa).

above right: *A Tamworth sow and piglets.*

below: *The skeleton and main feathers of a sparrow hawk. Six months after this bird died, only the principal bones remain.*

Chickens

The Iron Age farmers may also have kept chickens. The evidence is very slim indeed, but if they did it would have been the Indian red jungle fowl. This fowl is the predecessor of all the modern varieties of chickens. Caesar mentions that chickens and geese were kept, but because bird bones are so frail very few have survived. However, as archaeological techniques improve and more and more objects are found, perhaps more of the tiny bird bones may be discovered. On the other hand, it is easy to test how unlikely it would be for bird bones to survive by burying the carcass of a chicken in the ground, leaving it for a year and then digging it up again very carefully. Many of the tiny bones will be destroyed by the acidity of the soil. In particular places, like certain bogs, bones are sometimes preserved. In excavations of Iron Age sites at Glastonbury and Meare in Somerset, large quantities of bird bones survived telling us that men hunted wild birds, probably with nets, snares and spears. It is likely that Iron Age farmers also hunted rabbits as well as birds and boars. Today we still do this.

Dogs

Dogs were also kept and we have evidence from the Roman writers that hunting dogs were exported from Britain. The bone evidence for dogs suggests that a number of types existed, but the hunting dog may well have looked like the Irish wolfhound. One famous skeleton of a dog which looks like a cross between a whippet and a greyhound was discovered at Maiden Castle in Dorset. Dog burials are quite common and often these burials are in special places like the entrances to settlements and hill forts, but why this should be so we shall never know. Perhaps the dog, like the horse, was regarded as an important animal.

Bees

Finally it is likely that the farmer kept bees in order to have regular supplies of honey. Sugar, of course, was unknown in prehistoric or Roman times, and some sort of sweetener would have been necessary if only in the making of beer. We know that the Romans were good bee-keepers because several guides to bee-keeping have survived, especially one written by the poet Virgil. What kind of bees existed in Iron Age Britain is almost impossible to tell but certainly they would have been different from the modern varieties which have been specially bred. Experts think they may have been quite small, and fiercer than modern bees. All the same it is reasonable to think of the farmer having a group of hives and carefully collecting the honey at the right season and storing it away in pots. Perhaps one day evidence for bee-keeping will be discovered, perhaps a wing encased in some substance, maybe even bits of a hive if the conditions are right. Because no major structures would be required, nor specialist tools needed, the archaeological evidence must be very scarce indeed.

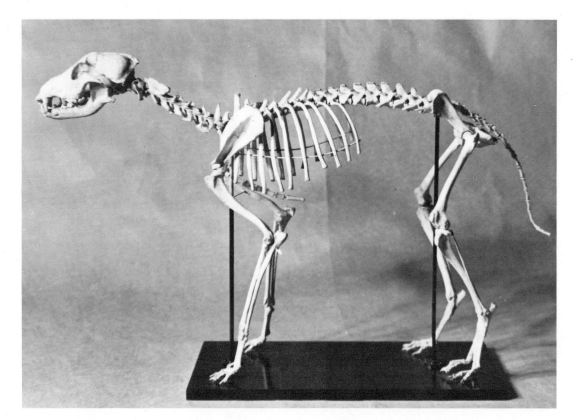

The skeleton of a dog found during excavations of the Iron Age settlement on Maiden Castle in Dorset.

3 SUMMER

Once spring is over, the lambing finished, and crops planted, you might expect there to be a quiet period of time before the harvest in late summer. So it might seem, but in farming there are very few quiet periods and this time is certainly not one of them. Farming, in a very simple and fundamental sense, is the provision of foodstuff for men and animals throughout the year. Therefore, while there is an abundance of food in the growing season, man has to work extremely hard to grow, collect and preserve food for the other times of the year.

Hay

Because we know that the Iron Age farmer used oxen to draw the ards and carts, we saw that he also had to provide winter food supplies for the oxen. The same argument may be used for all his other animals, including sheep, goats and pigs. There is no clear evidence of what food he collected and stored, but it is reasonable to think that hay was the easiest and best kind of food. In the early summer, therefore, haymaking would be a major activity. Some fields would have been specially kept for their grass. They may even have been manured in the preceding autumn to improve the quality of the grass. The best time for haymaking is just before the grass flowers. Then it must be cut and sun-dried in rows. Often it is necessary to turn the grass over so that the sun can dry it thoroughly; otherwise when it is stacked it will become overheated and may burst into flame. In some years when the weather is right it is possible to make two hay crops, in May and again in July. The major principle in making hay is to dry the grass so carefully that it stays green rather than turns brown. The greener it is the more food value it contains.

Haymaking tools

How could we prove that hay was made in the prehistoric period? What tools would have been necessary and what structures would have been needed? Unfortunately we have not yet discovered any scythes or large sickles, but is it likely that we would? Sickles made for cutting grass are usually very fine iron-bladed tools which would more readily rust away. In practice the usual thing that happens is if a tool like a sickle or a scythe is broken, the pieces are made into other tools. The point of a scythe easily becomes a splendid knife; the broad part of the blade can be used as a draw knife for stripping bark from fresh cut timber or for splitting logs. The parts of a sickle can in the same way be made into other edged tools. In farming we rarely throw away a tool just because it is broken and useless for its original purpose. In the Roman period we know they used scythes in Britain, but from the whole of the country fewer than

Sometimes in wet climates the cut grass is piled on to an upright stake to dry. The photograph shows how this is done today in Switzerland.

Building a haystack

1. *A simple rack supported by four posts to protect the bottom of the stack from damp.*

2. *The hay is piled on to the rack around a central pole.*

3. *A prefabricated thatched roof which can be used for many years.*

4. *The thatched roof in position on top of the haystack. The roof keeps the hay dry.*

twenty have been found so far. Therefore the absence of the metal tools cannot be regarded as strong evidence against an activity. Wooden tools, too, would not have survived except in very special circumstances. On page 47 you can see an example of a wooden fork which has been made recently from a young ash tree. Nature, in fact, provides a huge range of such tools, and it is always worth looking around for such examples. We can be sure that the Iron Age farmers were always on the look-out for shapes of timber which could be made into tools which relied upon the natural strength of the grain.

Stacks and racks

Archaeological evidence for built structures consists of post-holes and pits. What sort of evidence would a haystack leave? Sometimes round haystacks were built around a central post set in the ground. The evidence for such a stack would be just one solitary post-hole with perhaps a shallow depression around it. Such evidence is comparatively common. But it is not absolutely necessary to have a post in the middle. Its purpose is to allow the heat in the middle of the stack to escape. A simple tripod of poles would be just as effective and leave no evidence in the ground at all. So, we cannot prove that hay-making went on in the Iron Age but neither can we disprove it. Because cattle and sheep have to be fed in the winter it seems reasonable to believe that hay was made.

Some of the arrangements of four post-holes might represent hay barns and it has been suggested that pairs of post-holes could indicate drying racks for grass. However some of these post-hole pairs are so large, and would have taken such massive posts, that using them for drying grass is unlikely. Besides, it is much better to dry the grass on the fields, as the picture on page 19 shows.

Silage

Another winter animal food made from cut grass is silage. Scientific analysis of chemical deposits found in pits may help to solve the question of whether it was made in the Iron Age. Making silage is really quite simple. The grass is cut and then put into a pit and covered up with soil. Today molasses is added to the mixture, but the real process of grass preservation is caused by a bacterium which lives on the grass. When the

A reconstruction of a storage barn with a timber and turf roof.

grass is sealed into a pit the bacterium manufactures an acid which preserves the food value of the grass. In fact the process is the same as pickling onions in vinegar. You can read more about storage pits on page 43.

Vetch

There is another possible animal food. Carbonized seeds from a plant called vetch have been found, suggesting that it may have been specially cultivated. If it was grown it could well have been a food supply for both animals and humans, but especially for cattle. If planted at the right time it will grow well enough in the winter to provide grazing or forage in January and February, which are the worst months of all.

All these are ways in which the Iron Age farmer may have provided winter food for his animals, ways which would have demanded his attention during the early and middle summer. One day we may obtain sufficient evidence from excavations to be sure, and perhaps with better techniques we may discover evidence for even more kinds of food and farming processes.

Another task that would have taken much of the farmer's time during the summer would have been the building or repairing of his houses. The Iron Age farmstead needs a chapter to itself.

4 THE FARMSTEAD

The buildings

There are many questions still to be answered about how the Iron Age farmer lived. Even though some evidence of his settlements is available it is not possible to say how many people lived in large groups or small, or what kind of sites they preferred for their buildings.

The archaeologist must begin by patiently trying to reconstruct post-hole patterns into three-dimensional houses. This is extremely difficult; we have to remember that even if the buildings we create 'feel' right, they are only the result of careful detective work and can easily be wrong if the evidence is inadequate.

Reconstructing a stone house

The photographs show three stages in the building of a stone roundhouse with a thatched roof. Although it looks simple it is a very complex building relying upon natural stresses and strains, leather lashing and simple wood joints.

The quantity of material used in its construction is not small: fifty tons of limestone, four tons of hay and straw, two tons of timber.

The stone had to be dug up and transported, probably in carts, to the site of the house. Then it had to be laid into a wall without any cement. The trees had to be selected, cut down, trimmed and carried to the site. Hazel rods or slender willow branches (withes) had to be cut, bundled and transported. In fact it is likely that hazel trees and willow trees were specially grown to provide the right sort of timber for house building, fence building and basket making. The skins of animals also had to be scraped and prepared, cut into strips and soaked before being used. Finally straw had to be gathered at harvest time, bundled properly and stored until it was needed. Thatching straw is usually best after it has been kept for a year. All these activities would require considerable amounts of effort and time and a great deal of skill.

Once all the materials are concentrated at the building site, the construction can go ahead. In fact the building time can be quite short, a matter of two or three weeks only from start to

In Spain today some farmers still use ox-drawn carts with wooden wheels.

right: *The foundation trench with edging stones in place.*

far right: *The completed dry stone wall.*

An early stage in the thatching process. You can see the completed house in the picture on page 44.

finish. But the process is so complex we must wonder if there were specialist builders at work, just as there are today. The farmer really would have had very little time to spare to build houses and may not have possessed the skills required.

The tools available during the Iron Age were wide ranging. We can be sure that apart from the jack plane, a full carpenter's tool kit existed then. The saw is especially interesting because it worked on the opposite principle to the modern saw. The cutting teeth worked on the pull action whereas the modern saw teeth cut on the push stroke. Many of the carpenter's jobs for which we use specialist tools, a craftsman is able to do with an axe. It is quite amazing how quickly a delicate joint can be made with an axe in the right hands. (There are pictures of tools on pages 47 and 48.)

Reconstructing a wooden house

A different kind of house can be seen in these photographs. The evidence for this house suggested that it was made from stakes driven into a shallow gully with the wall consisting of hazel rods or willow withes interwoven between the stakes. The only substantial post-holes form the porch of the house and are very necessary to the strength of this house. Its construction is similar to a wicker shopping basket but the doorway represents a break in the circle. It needs to be strengthened considerably so that the weight of the roof will not break down the walls. It is easy to understand the strength of basketry by standing on the edge of a shopping basket. Basically weak material when

1. *The shallow circular gulley with prepared stakes.*

2. *Half of the stakes have been driven into position.*

3. *The completed wall framework.*

4. *Detail of wickerwork.*

5. *The apex of the roof.*

6. *The main rafters in position.*

7. *Detail of the ring beam.*

interwoven together makes an enormously strong shape. Any break in the basket promptly reduces its strength.

The roof structure is equally simple and very similar to that of the stone house. At first three rafters are tied together at the narrow ends, raised to the vertical position with the tied point in the air and the 'legs' walked out to form a tripod. This tripod is lifted on to the top of the walls and lashed into position. Another three rafters are added to the tripod and these few rafters form the principal element of the roof. At this stage the roof is quite weak and could easily be broken down.

The problem now lies in the top part or apex of the cone. Many more rafters will distort the roof shape at the apex and make it awkward to thatch properly. Therefore a ring of withes tied into a hoop is placed over the apex and tied to the main rafters. All the other rafters are now tied to the ring and to the wall. This ring, or heep, is called a ring beam. As each rafter is added so the roof becomes stronger and stronger until, when the withes are interwoven between the rafters, it is possible to climb all over the roof. The thatching process again is as simple

The first layer of yealms tied in place.

The interior of a thatched roof looking into the apex.

as possible. Bundles of straw called yealms are tied into place, working from the eaves to the apex as shown in the diagram.

The final stage of building is the application of daub to the walls. Daub is a mixture of clay, soil, roots, straw, hay, grass, animal hair and possibly cow dung in careful proportions. Pure clay would dry out and crack and fall away from the walls, and mud would just wash away. Often in excavations fragments of burnt daub are found which still retain the marks of the hazel or willow rods. Putting the daub on to the walls is a splendid job. Once the mix is satisfactory, with a consistency of moist modeling clay, lumps of it are hurled against the wall and then pressed on to make sure that the daub fits snugly into the woodwork. Then the walls are smoothed over just like the plaster in a modern house. The final layer may have been a thin coating of clay mixed with cow dung. Dung gives an admirable weather proof protective layer. Perhaps this final layer was also decorated with patterns and designs.

An alternative method of thatching

Layers of straw are laid on to the roof and fixed down with split rods held in place by spars. A spar, approximately 60 cm (2 feet) long, is used just like a staple. The tool, probably a spar hook, is used for splitting the hazel rods lengthwise. (Shown here at one eighth actual size.)

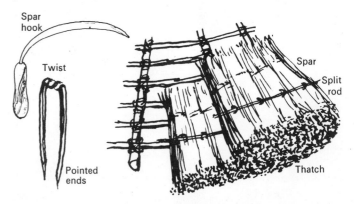

Spar hook

Twist

Pointed ends

Spar

Split rod

Thatch

Daubing the wall of a roundhouse.

These two houses are based upon plans of two particularly good excavations where great care was paid to every detail during the digging process. Working from such good plans means that our basic evidence is more easily understood so that the reconstructions are reasonable and more likely to be true. There are many advantages to be gained by building such houses. One of the most important is the way in which we can see the real size, and understand the great skill that went into the building of it, for these are not crude huts. Another advantage is that the reconstructions help us to understand archaeological evidence in three dimensions.

However, there are a great number of variations in the basic evidence for roundhouses. Some have post-built walls, others seem to be made of cob (a mixture of chalk and clay), others again of turf (sod). In fact the variety of materials used in the Iron Age is similar to the variety used today. Size of houses also varies enormously; some were quite small, 4-5 metres (about 5 yards) in diameter, while others were huge at 15 metres (over 16 yards) in diameter. A modern house would fit inside the largest Iron Age houses.

How were the buildings used?

The kind of house and the number of houses inside a farmstead varied considerably. We really do not have a great deal of good evidence yet. Another problem we need to solve is what the houses were used for. Did all the household activities go on inside one house or were they spread about two or three houses? For example, one house could have been used for daily activities, cooking, eating and talking, while another may have been a special weaving house, and yet another set aside for sleeping. Maybe cattle were kept inside a roundhouse either on their own or with the people. Perhaps in time we shall discover these answers as we think more carefully about how to improve excavations. At present we can only guess.

The layout of the farmstead

The farmstead itself is also quite difficult to describe. Usually an area was surrounded with a ditch and bank, with a palisade fence set into the top of the bank. Exactly why they dug out the ditches and built the banks is a difficult question to answer. The ditches are hardly deep and wide enough to be militarily useful and seem to be better understood as animal barriers. Often the ditch and bank are described as fences against wild animals but such barriers would rarely stop a determined wild animal. Perhaps they are simple fence lines showing the ownership rights of the farmer. One function they do serve well is to give the farmstead area some protection from the wind. Most of the farmsteads so far discovered are on high ground, and some way of blunting the power of the wind would be very desirable.

Excavation inside the farmstead area often reveals a maze of post-holes and pits which show evidence of occupation. Sometimes the post-holes seem to form patterns, as for example, the plans of roundhouses. Occasionally an isolated group of post-holes is found which suggests a rectangular building. A reconstruction of a 'barn' based upon such a pattern can be seen on page 21. But it is almost impossible to guess what sort of structure may have existed there. One extremely important way of discovering possible answers is to 'reconstruct the event'. In other words we need to build and operate an Iron Age farmstead in order to find out what would have been necessary. In this way the needs of the farming process will suggest

A reconstruction of a ditch and bank with palisade fence.

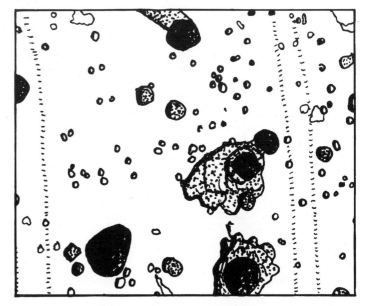

A maze of post-holes as recorded in an excavation of an Iron Age site.

interpretations for the archaeological evidence. (This is what is being done at the Butser Ancient Farm Research Project in Hampshire.) For example, we know that fences are necessary in any farming process. Evidence suggests that Iron Age farmers may have used wattle hurdles, portable fence panels made of interwoven branches. A wattle hurdle maker erects two parallel rails supported by two posts against which he leans the hazel rods used in the hurdle while he works in the central area. All that remains archaeologically of his activity are four post-holes. Yet the post-holes are similar to those of a real structure and the archaeologist has no way of finding out which was which. The range of possible answers will gradually increase as the problems are faced.

top: *A wattle hurdle fence and* (below) *a fence of continuous interwoven timbers.*

Work about the farmstead

Fires and cooking

Inside the homes we have found evidence of domestic activities and already it is possible to think of Iron Age 'home economics'. Cooking is a vital part of each and every day, and we have to discover how the people cooked, what they cooked and what kind of household utensils they possessed. Straight away we need to forget all the popular stories of the strange and crude diets of prehistoric man.

The 'how' of cooking is a fascinating subject. Archaeologists have discovered the remains of two types of oven, one a clay dome baking oven which has a world-wide distribution, the other a variation of it consisting of a fire compartment in the bottom of the dome with a cooking compartment above it. So we know they could have baked bread in the baking oven. To do this the oven must be thoroughly heated with a charcoal fire. It has to be a charcoal fire because inside the dome the oxygen supply is too low for ordinary wood to burn. Once the whole oven is hot the embers are raked out and the dough popped in to cook from the remaining heat. The second oven can be used in the same way as a modern oven.

A reconstructed bread oven made of clay.

There is also the ordinary hearth fire consisting of a level layer of embers and ashes on which pots can be boiled and above which meat can be roasted. It is worth remembering that there are four basic forms of fire which are regularly used in the service of man. The best known is the bonfire which is built with dry wood piled up in the shape of a pyramid or wigwam. This will give out a tremendous amount of heat and flame but does not last very long. It is the normal kind of fire for disposing of rubbish, and in time gone by it was regularly used as a beacon fire. A variation of the pyramid fire but much longer lasting is the pagoda fire. The other fires are basically cooking fires and their names derive from their shape: the star fire, the parallel fire and finally the pit, or trench, fire. The pictures show what these are like.

Because the normal forms of cooking were available, it is only sensible to assume that they were used. One excellent variation of baking not normally used today could have been a regular method of food preparation in the Iron Age. Small animals and fish can be encased in clay and baked for an hour or so in the heart of the fire. The clay coating keeps all the juices in and preserves the succulence of the meat. When it is cooked the clay is broken away, and as it breaks it takes the skin of the animal too, leaving the meat all ready to eat. It is a favourite way of cooking hedgehogs, the meat of which is absolutely delicious.

It has often been suggested that the prehistoric diet was dull and monotonous, with a basic dish of porridge and nettle broth. The evidence, on the other hand, suggests the opposite. As the full range of cooking facilities existed, so did a varied and rewarding diet. The latest research on prehistoric cereals and vegetables is proving that a much higher protein level was present than in modern foods. In fact, the protein level is often more than twice the modern figure. It is only necessary for us to consider the normal variety of foods available then from the livestock of the farm, and to add the range of wild animals, fish and birds, fruits and roots in order to come to the conclusion that our own diet is stolid and comparatively dull. How many people today have tasted spit-roasted suckling pig, stone-

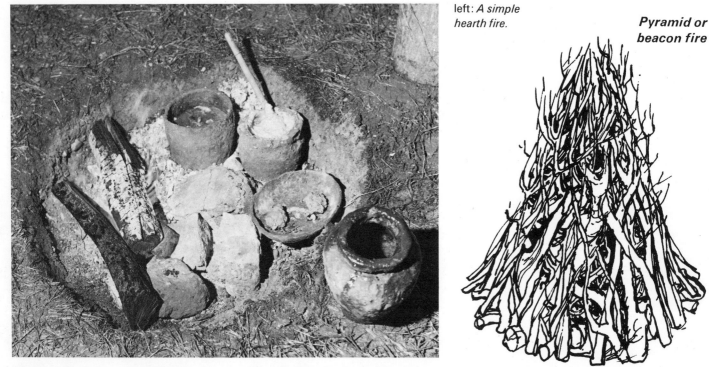

left: *A simple hearth fire.*

Pyramid or beacon fire

ground emmer bread, fresh wild raspberries and shellfish, mature beef, nut-sweet Celtic beans, boiled melde? The list is almost without end, and in this company even nettle broth is not unattractive.

One important element for the cooking process and for general food preservation, especially meat, is salt. In Iron Age Britain we believe that salt panning was carried out around the coastline and then transported and traded to the inland people. Exactly how this was done is not known at present. On a farmstead large quantities of salt would inevitably be required, especially in the autumn when fresh meat would be 'salted down', probably in pits for use during the winter. Salt producing must have been a full-time light industry.

Enjoying a clay-baked fish.

Parallel fire

This can also be set in a shallow trench.
The closer the logs, the higher the flame.

Pagoda fire

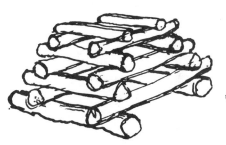

Star fire

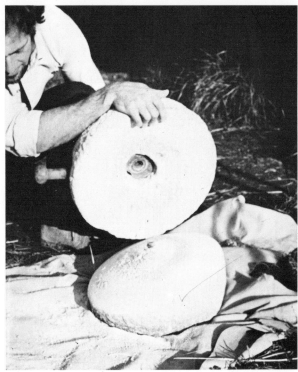

above: *A saddle quern.*

right: *A rotary quern. The bottom stone is fixed. The upper stone, rotating on a wooden pin, grinds the grain which is dribbled in through a central hole in the top stone.*

Utensils

Food preparation leaves remarkably few traces apart from the tools needed, and these were hardly specialist items. However a regular find on excavations is the quern stone, used to grind the wheat and other hard seeds into flour. In the early part of the Iron Age the saddle quern was in common use but this was later replaced by the rotary quern. The fact that querns are made of stone is what accounts for their survival. Often they are broken and have been thrown away and rarely are both parts of the quern found. But even if we had no other evidence for food apart from quern stones, we would be able to deduce that grain was grown, harvested and ground into flour, and suspect that the flour was made into bread.

Pottery vessels are quite common. Again rarely does an archaeologist find a complete pot. Usually only fragments of pottery are found. These have to be painstakingly cleaned and recorded, and matching pieces are fitted together in the hope that the original shape and possible use may be discovered. In fact dealing with the broken pieces or sherds of pottery is a similar detective process to the interpretation of post-holes and pits. Sometimes the sherds give hints as to a special function; for example some have special lugs to hang the pot from, and others have lots of holes suggesting the pot was originally a colander or strainer of some kind. If colanders or strainers existed it is reasonable to think that cheese was made. Even a tiny piece of evidence like a sherd can suggest an activity.

What does the manufacture of cheese mean? First of all, milk must be produced. Therefore cows, goats or sheep were kept and either all or some of them were milked. This, in turn, means all the problems associated with animal care, and adds a further element to the diet. Often this kind of argument can be carried too far, but it does show how necessary it is to work through a process for oneself. By doing so we may find new pieces of evidence which had previously been overlooked.

Making pottery

Pottery-making itself is an enormous problem. Archaeologists are not at all sure how pottery was fired. Many theories exist, but very few have been properly tested. Gradually information is being gathered together. Experts have concentrated on what the pottery was made of and, by analysis of the clay and specks of stone, have sometimes been able to tell where the raw materials came from. They can also work out the proportions of the clay and stone fragments.

By looking at other peasant cultures of today, where pottery is made by the people themselves rather than by an industrial process, we can get some idea of how it was made in the Iron Age. But the evidence from the modern processes must agree with the archaeological evidence.

Making pottery is not as easy as it looks. Two basic methods for hand-made pottery, like that of most of the iron Age, are known. The first is called the ball, or lump, method. Clay and finely crushed stone fragments are mixed together and kneaded or 'wedged' until the mixture has the consistency of moist modeling clay. It is then made into a ball. By pressing the thumbs into the middle of the ball, the potter makes the first shape of the pot. Thereafter, by squeezing out the sides evenly and taking special care to maintain the same thickness, the required shape can be made. The potter must never let the clay become crumbly while working it.

The second method is to wedge the clay as before and then make it into rolls which can be coiled around a disc base. By building the coils up and carefully working them together to squeeze out all the air and make a solid wall, very large pots indeed can be made. Huge storage vessels as big as a human were made in this way by the Cretans.

Pots made by both methods can be polished or burnished by rubbing them all over with, perhaps, a smooth piece of bone. Any hard, smooth-surfaced object will do. The burnishing helps to compact the fabric of the pot.

In order to fire a pot, clay has to be heated to a temperature of not less than 600°C and ideally about 900°C. Usually this is done in a pottery kiln, but hardly any evidence of pottery kilns from Iron Age Britain has yet been recognized. In Denmark several simple kilns have been found and one is described later in this chapter.

It is possible to reach these high temperatures in a bonfire

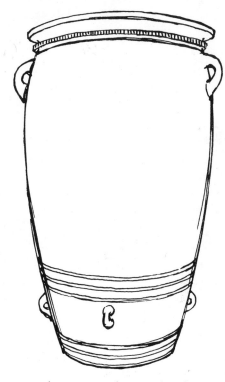

A storage pot from ancient Crete.

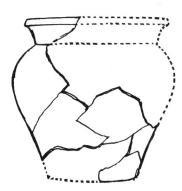

The shape of an Iron Age pot, as worked out from small fragments.

An early stage in the building of a pit clamp. More wood and a turf covering are yet to be added.

but the heat is usually uncontrolled and too varied in intensity. However, if a bonfire is built and then covered with turf blocks, the temperature can be controlled to a certain extent. This is called a clamp fire. If this clamp fire is built in a shallow pit, it works even better. It is then called a pit clamp.

The process of firing pottery in a pit clamp is easier than actually making the pots themselves. First, a shallow circular depression approximately 0.45 metres (18 inches) by 0.15 metres (6 inches) deep is scooped out of the ground and lined with dry straw or hay. The dried pots are piled carefully into this depression to form a pyramid. Twigs and small pieces of dry wood are stacked around the pots until they are completely covered. Then larger and greener timbers are stacked up until the fire measures about 1 metre (3 feet 4 inches) diameter and is about 1 metre high, although it is still roughly shaped like a pyramid. Two cracks in the timber are left on either side to give space to set fire to the straw at the bottom. The whole of the fire is covered completely with fresh-cut turf. All the cracks between the blocks of turf are filled with soil. A reserve stack of turf needs to be kept at hand. Once the straw has been lit and the fire is burning well, the potter must quickly cover up the remaining cracks in the turf cover. The pit clamp needs to be watched carefully for the first few hours. Every time the fire burns through the turf, more blocks must be placed on.

After at least twenty-four hours, and ideally much longer so that the clamp is quite cold, the potter breaks it open carefully and takes out the fired pots. Sometimes the pots have a fine ash glaze, sometimes patches of red; occasionally pots are broken during the firing. As with all skills, practice is important. The charcoal could burst into flames when the clamp is opened. This, apart from being dangerous, could well spoil the pots. This system of making pottery, called reduction firing, usually turns all the pots black because the fire burns without oxygen. The occasional red patches on the fired pots show where oxygen was leaked into the fire.

From excavations in Denmark we have an example of a simple pottery kiln. It consists of a hollow dug out of a slope and covered with a clay hood. The pots are placed on the shelf at the back of the kiln. A small fire is started in the fire box at the front of the kiln and gradually built up over two or three hours until it completely fills the kiln mouth. Then a wall of stone blocks is built across the mouth of the kiln, and the cracks between the blocks are thoroughly caulked with moist clay. Three small holes are left in this wall to allow the draft through. Once the clay pots, which can be seen through the chimney hole, glow red, the correct firing temperature of just over 700°C has been achieved. It is vital to take great care when checking the pottery through the chimney because the heat is intense.

A kiln firing can be either reducing, making black pottery, or oxidizing, making red pottery. A kiln is much harder work to fire than a pit clamp because wood has to be fed into the fire box for a long time before the kiln can be left to cool and the pots removed from the firing shelf.

Bonfires, of course, do leave a burned area, but this is easily lost or destroyed by later activity. Although bonfiring pottery is done today, this is usually in hot countries where it is possible to dry out the pot completely before it is fired. Any moisture left in the clay will cause the pot to explode when it is fired. Britain rarely has weather hot enough to guarantee that the pot will be properly dry, since clay will absorb moisture even if the atmosphere is only slightly damp.

All this leads the archaeologist to two conclusions. First, the pit clamp is a more likely method in Britain than the bonfire. Second, the pottery fabric is important. If fragments of burned flint or stone are mixed with the clay when the pot is made, the flint or stone will absorb the heat of the fire faster and help to

Building a kiln

1. *The hollow is dug out of a slope.*

2. *The wicker-work framework supports the clay cover. When fired, the wood burns away completely.*

3. *Building the clay cover.*

4. *The completed kiln seen from the front. Note the air control holes and 'ash-box'.*

5. *Section drawing of the completed kiln.*

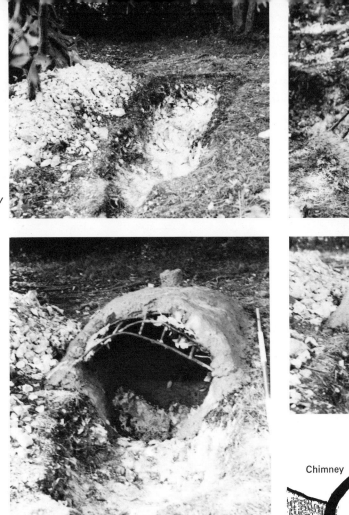

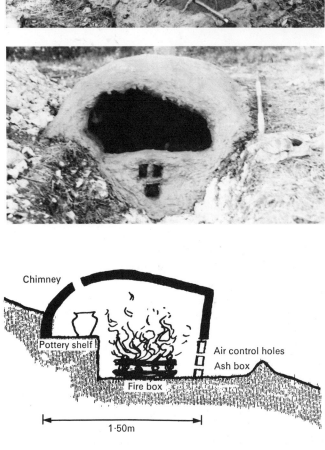

Chimney

Pottery shelf

Air control holes

Ash box

Fire box

1·50m

dry out the last bit of moisture in the clay. Because the pit clamp heats up more slowly than a bonfire the pots are less likely to explode. The same argument applies to the kiln where the fire can be made very gradually indeed. Although the pictures of the kiln show it set into the ground, it is quite possible to build it so that it sits on the surface of the ground. The evidence we would find would again be an intensively burned out confined area, and lumps of fired clay from the kiln structure. Such lumps of

Three pots which had been fired in an experimental pit clamp. They are not Iron Age types.

This gold torc, or twisted necklace, was found in Snettisham, England.

The bowl of a wooden ladle from the Glastonbury lake village. Width 8.9 cm (3½ inches).

clay would look exactly like burnt daub from a house wall, and the burned area like a hearth. Perhaps the evidence is there but we have not recognized it.

Pottery in the Iron Age is really quite crude and not at all attractive like the beautiful metalwork of the period. Because the pottery is so poor, there is good reason to believe that a lot of the household utensils were made of wood. Some extremely fine examples of woodworking have been found, like the ladle from the Glastonbury and Meare lake villages. The conclusions about woodwork are difficult to prove because wood does not last long enough. We have evidence for wooden buckets and stave barrels, both of which suggest considerable carpentry skills. One of the most difficult things to make is a water-tight stave barrel. There may well have been specialist carpenters who made only such objects and utensils. Pottery on the other hand would probably have been part of the domestic industry of the farm, and if this is right it was almost certainly a summer occupation.

5 AUTUMN

The harvest

In late summer and early autumn, the long hot days when the crops ripen, the Iron Age farmers would be preparing for one of the busiest and most important times of the year. Harvest time brings the fruits of all their labours. Plowing the fields in the cold winds of autumn and spring, sowing the seed, the endless hoeing of the weeds, all lead to the ultimate purpose of the harvest. Now the farmers have to plan carefully first the harvest itself, the labour required, the equipment for reaping, carting, and finally storing the seeds. So many plants, both domestic and wild, bear fruit at this time of year and the days are never long enough to accomplish all that needs to be done.

The cereal crops are the most important. Our evidence comes from the finds of carbonized seeds and seed impressions in pottery (as explained on pages 10 and 11), and it is from these that we can identify the wheats and barleys that were grown. The first to ripen is the winter-sown barley, followed by the wheats, emmer and spelt, their long awns making them look more like barley than like any modern wheat. Finally spring-sown crops ripen in due order, allowing time for the collection of all the different kinds of cereals. Exactly which cereals were winter varieties and which were spring varieties is still to be established by research experiments. In addition we have no real ideas of the sort of yields the Iron Age farmers would have expected. Gradually this information will be obtained by actually growing these cereals and measuring the results. Already some figures are available which suggest that the prehistoric farmers were extremely efficient.

Reaping grain

We have two important pieces of evidence that help us to reconstruct the process of reaping. A classical writer tells us that the Celtic peoples in the Iron Age reaped their grain by cutting

Spelt wheat
(Triticum spelte)

Emmer wheat
(Triticum dicoccum)

A typical sickle of the Iron Age, shown here at one eighth actual size.

it just below the ear. In fact this method of reaping is still used in a remote area high in the mountains of northern Spain. Secondly, small hand sickles are quite often found on excavations of Iron Age settlement sites. Experiments with the small sickles show that it is a very good way of reaping even if it is hard work. It is good because only the ears of wheat, and no other seeds, can be collected. Perhaps we should picture the farmers, first of all sharpening all the sickles and making sure that the sacks they wore like aprons were clean and ready without any holes in them. Then on the day when reaping was due to begin they would anxiously test the grains in the time-honoured fashion of biting through the seed. When the seed is ready it is hard all the way through and more or less the same colour. If the seed goes beyond this stage, it will begin to fall out of the ear and be lost. Before this stage the seed is white and soft and will not grind up easily into flour. Once they were satisfied that the grain was ready and the early morning sun had dried away the dew, they would give the word to the workers. The sacks would have been put on and the reaping commenced. Everyone from the youngest to the oldest on the farmstead must have helped at harvest time.

Straw

The harvested seed would then be brought back to the farmstead for the next stage of treatment. But work in the field was far from over. The standing straw, now without the ears of grain, was extremely valuable and could not have been left to rot. It was necessary for thatching, animal feed, and bedding for humans and animals. It is reasonable to think that it was carefully cut and bundled up into sheaves or yealms and tied with twisted straw ropes. The bundles would then be carted back to the farmstead and stored in a barn or out-house of some kind until they were needed.

The drawing shows how the ears of wheat only are cut off.

Emmer wheat ready to be harvested.

Woad (Isatis tinctoria)

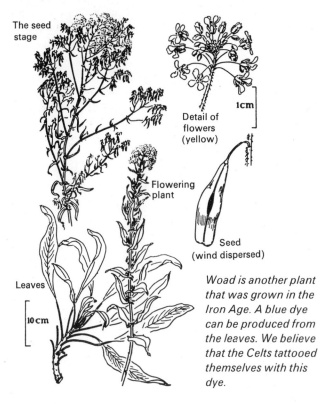

The seed stage

Detail of flowers (yellow)

1cm

Flowering plant

Seed (wind dispersed)

Leaves

10 cm

Woad is another plant that was grown in the Iron Age. A blue dye can be produced from the leaves. We believe that the Celts tattooed themselves with this dye.

Celtic bean (Vicia faba minor)

We are not at all sure how the grain was threshed. The seed from both emmer wheat and spelt wheat does not easily fall from the ear. Perhaps it was crushed in order to loosen the seed and then winnowed.

Preparing the fields

Finally the fields would need to be prepared again for the next season. The first job after the straw had been cut and taken away was to plow the land lightly and then spread manure over it to put back some of the nutrients taken out by the cereal crop. It is so easy to say this in a very few words, but the physical process requires many back-breaking hours raking out the manure from the manure pile, forking it into carts or sleds, dragging it out to the fields and then spreading it on the land. As well as the fields that had grown cereals, probably the grass fields too were manured, so that the pasture could be improved.

The bean harvest

Once the cereal harvest was in, the beans were ready to be picked. Probably they were used as a vegetable throughout the season, as we use the modern varieties ourselves, but the important crop of beans came when the seed was hard and the germ fixed. Then they could be easily stored for food and a proportion kept for seed in the following spring. The bean plants would have been cut down and probably fed to the pigs. It was important to leave the roots of the bean plant in the ground, because the nitrogen nodule needs to be left there to enrich the soil. (Even if the farmer did not know about nitrogen, he probably did know that the beans improved the soil.)

The melde crop

Perhaps the melde crop was also harvested at this time. We are not entirely sure that it was a field crop in the Iron Age, but if it was, the seed would have been ready in late September and would need to be harvested as carefully as the rest of the crops. It is fascinating to think that bread might have been made from melde seed as well as from the conventional cereals. Certainly its food value is very high. The green leaves and the fruit make a splendid vegetable, though this is more a seasonal plant than an all-year-round food.

Planting vetch

At this time, too, the farmers may well have planted a vetch crop to provide some winter forage for their cattle. By timing the planting carefully they could have ensured a regular food supply of green stuff through the bad winter months. However, the first concern was to plant the winter cereals in the plowed fields before the onset of the autumn frosts. We are not sure how precisely the farmers timed the seasons of the year, but it is most likely that they used the stars for their guide just as the Romans did. The night sky was probably as important to farmers as it was to sailors.

While all this activity of reaping, plowing and winter sowing was going ahead at full pressure, there was yet an even more urgent task to be attended to. The harvested cereal had to be stored away so that it would not deteriorate.

Melde or 'fat hen' (Chenopodium album)

Vetch (Vicia sativa)

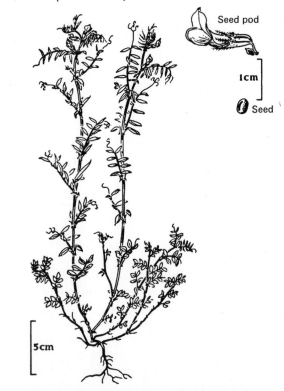

Flowers

Seed pods

1cm

5mm

Seed

10cm

Seed pod

1cm

Seed

5cm

right: *The pit is dug into chalk rock.*

far right: *The pit is filled with grain. The wires and tubes are inserted to record temperatures and gas concentrations.*

The clay makes a gas- and water-tight seal for the grain.

Storing the grain

There are a number of very important problems for us to solve before we can really understand what food the Iron Age farmer produced and what he did with it. For example, we believe the farmer was very efficient and probably grew more grain than he could use himself. What did he do with the surplus? One answer is given to us by a classical writer who says that grain was exported from Britain to the continent. While this explains where the surplus might have gone it does not tell us how it was exported. Was the grain exported for food consumption or was it seed grain? When was it exported, in the autumn or in the spring? The autumn is a time of intense activity on the farm and the problems of moving the harvest, added to all the other work, may have been too much to do at one time.

The archaeological evidence does help a little at this point, as does another comment from a classical writer. The written evidence tells us that the Celts stored the grain in underground pits. Excavation has revealed many huge pits on large numbers of Iron Age settlements. The pits are particularly common on chalk and limestone areas and in the river valleys of sand and gravel. Working from these two pieces of evidence archaeologists have conducted experiments.

The theory of storing grain is really quite simple. Like a human being, grain uses up oxygen and gives off carbon dioxide in its normal respiration or living process. If the grain is put inside a sealed container it will quickly use up all the oxygen present. Then it stops growing and becomes dormant until more oxygen is introduced. The pit works just like a sealed container. A hole dug into the rock, sometimes up to 2 metres (6 feet) deep by 1 metre (3 feet) in diameter, is filled with grain and a seal of moist clay covered by loose soil is put on top. The loose soil keeps the clay moist and so stops any penetration by rainwater. However, things can still go wrong inside the pit because tiny organisms called bacteria and fungi are present on the seeds of grain when they are put into the pit. There is no way

right: *Section diagram of a grain storage pit, 1 metre deep.*

far right: *Rubble capping over the clay seal.*

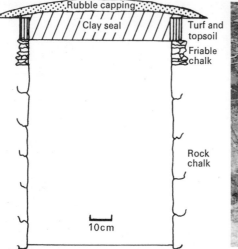

Rubble capping

Clay seal

Turf and topsoil

Friable chalk

Rock chalk

10 cm

right: *Recording the temperatures inside the storage pit.*

far right: *Analysing the gas concentrations.*

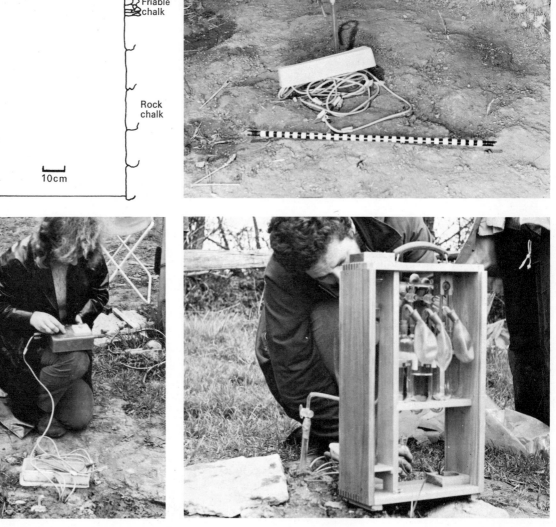

of getting rid of these organisms, but by controlling the conditions inside the pit their activity can be kept to a minimum. We have all seen how fungi will grow on a piece of cheese or bread if it is left for a time. The same thing can happen inside a pit. But neither fungi nor bacteria grow very well without oxygen, nor at a low temperature. As long as the grain is stored in a pit only during the winter when temperatures are low, then it can be stored successfully with little damage from these tiny organisms. Of course the Iron Age farmer did not know about bacteria but he could have found out by experiment the best way of keeping grain in good condition.

Recent experiments have proved that grain stored in this way

42

will still grow extremely well. So a pit could well have been the method of storing, especially for seed grain. It was once thought that grain stored in this way was for food and had to be dried first. Again experiments have shown that it is difficult to open a pit during the winter and then reseal it because each time the seal is broken oxygen is allowed in. This increases the possibilities of the grain in the pit going bad. An alternative is to open a pit and use all the contents, but this would mean using up perhaps two tons of grain at a time. Besides, it is much easier and more sensible to keep the relatively small quantities of grain needed for food in large pottery jars inside the home or barn. Examples of such jars have been found on several excavations.

Perhaps the pit is a kind of storage warehouse where the surplus is kept until it is needed either for sowing the following year or for trade. There is more time for recovering and moving the stored grain from the pits just before the spring begins.

Because of the low constant temperature to be found underground other foodstuffs could also have been stored in underground pits. Beans, for example, could have been kept in this way. Some pits could have been used as larders for salted meat. But not all the pits that are excavated on Iron Age sites are for food storage. Indeed most pits may have had other uses.

Some pits may have been lined with clay and used especially for water collection. Some of the shallow pits could have been the stands for water barrels. Several pits have been found full of washed or prepared clay and are probably the 'clay bins' of potters who first cleaned the clay and then stored it in such a way as to let the clay weather over a period of months. Some other pits have been found filled with sling stones. These are described as 'arsenals'.

We know from classical writings that the British brewed a drink from grain, probably a type of beer. How did they discover the process? Experiments with grain storage pits may have shown the way. One winter the rainfall was so high that water penetrated into the pit and, of course, soaked the grain. In fact it did not spoil it completely because, although it would not grow, it was still edible. However, during the recovery of the wet grain from the pit, the people digging it became 'tipsy' or slightly drunk from the fumes. It is only a small step between smelling the liquid and tasting it. By adding honey the bitterness of the taste is lessened and the effect of drinking it is just the same as drinking modern beer.

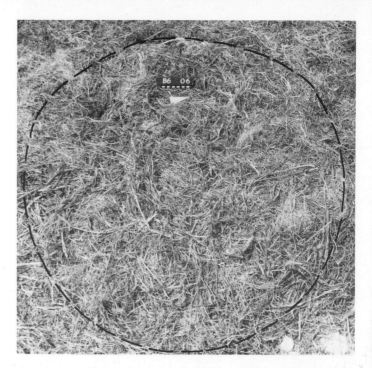

Another possible use for a pit is the manufacture of silage (see page 21). The above picture shows a pit filled with freshly cut grass. For the grass to cure, it is necessary to cover it completely with a heavy weight. Below, chalk blocks have been put on top of the grass.

6 WINTER

The winter was a slower time for the Iron Age farmer just as it is today. It was the time to take stock of the year, to maintain and repair the fences, build new ones, repair the tackle and choose the timber for new implements to be smoke-seasoned over the winter fire. There were still many jobs to be done but the pressure was eased. Once the grass stopped growing all the animals needed to be fed daily and carefully watched. It was the time of preparations for the coming season.

Making clothes

Perhaps during the winter time most of the spinning and weaving was done. We have a lot of archaeological evidence for the manufacture of clothes in the prehistoric period including, from Denmark, actual clothing recovered from the bogs. In the chapter on spring the Soay sheep were described, and we saw how, in the early summer, the wool was plucked rather than sheared.

Spinning

This wool is beautifully soft and spins easily into a soft yarn. A common find on excavations is the spindle whorl, a flat disc of stone or pottery with a central hole. A spindle is fitted into this hole as in the picture. The method of hand spinning has hardly altered at all to the present day and is not at all difficult. Depending on the size and weight of the spindle whorl, a thick or thin yarn can be spun.

First of all a quantity of wool is teased out with the fingers so that the fibres are loosely separated, and then a few fibres are twisted into a simple thread between the forefinger and thumb. Once this thread is long enough a slip knot is tied on to the notch on the spindle and this is twirled gently. It will rotate for quite a while and all the time, by teasing out the fibres of the wool, a person can spin a continuous thread. As the thread lengthens so the spindle reaches the floor and stops. In fact one can only spin at one time a length of yarn equal to the distance between the hands and the ground. The thread is then wound around the spindle and the process started again. Joins are made by fluffing out the end of the thread and twisting it into the unspun wool. After a little practice it is possible to produce a very fine and consistent yarn.

Weaving

Weaving, on the other hand, is a little more difficult and there is some argument about the precise details of loom designs. The archaeological evidence consists primarily of pear-shaped stone or clay weights, each with a hole drilled through the narrow end. Occasionally a number of these weights have been found in a line between two post-holes suggesting that an upright loom once stood in that position. The picture shows a simple upright

A spindle.

A clay loom weight. (One sixth actual size.)

below: *An upright loom. (In this picture the loom weights are not of Iron Age type.) The girl is making the yarn with a spindle.*

right: *The heddle bar opens the second shed.*

far right: *Beating up the weft with a wooden sword.*

A close-up picture of the woven cloth.

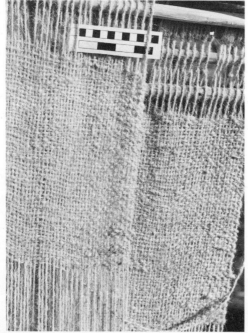

loom that works well. On the next page is a detailed view of the simplest kind of woven cloth that can be made on such a loom. The loom is a straightforward framework which supports the vertical threads, called the warp. The horizontal threads, called the weft, are interwoven between the vertical threads. The threads of the warp are tied on to the loom weights to keep them taut, and alternate threads are divided by a bar set into the lower part of the framework. The space thus created is called a shed, and allows the weft thread to be passed through. In order to achieve the interweaving process, each of the threads at the back of the shed is tied with loops through the threads of the front of the shed to a horizontal wooden bar called a heddle. By pulling this bar forward the back threads are pulled to the front and a second shed is formed. The weft is passed back through this second shed and thus forms the second row. The weaver makes the third row by releasing the heddle bar back to its original position, and again passing weft through the first shed. By steadily repeating this process cloth can quickly be made. Patterns are made by using different colours of wool and making different sheds. So mechanical can this process become that many weavers work better by touch than by sight. In the

long dark winter evenings, when the only light came from a simple oil lamp, this would be a desirable skill. (A modern comparison is the person who can knit quite intricate patterns without looking at the work at all.)

Woodwork

In the depths of winter there was still plenty of outdoor work to be done on the farmstead. At this time the farmer had to turn his attention to the woodland areas. Each farmstead must have had areas of woodland which were just as carefully maintained as any field. As we have seen wood was needed for much of the farmer's work. Certain trees needed regular attention. Hazel needed to be cut every year, to ensure a supply of rods to be made into hurdles, house walls, baskets, thatching spars and so on. For a regular supply of good hazel rods the farmer would need a seven-year plan because it takes that many years for a freshly cut hazel to grow useful timber. The process is called coppicing, and is best carried out when the sap is down and the wood dry. The same applies to all the trees in the woodland. You can see pictures of hazel coppicing on page 48.

It was undoubtedly at this time of year that the timber, principally oak, ash and elm, was cut and stockpiled to air-season before being used. It is interesting to record that the modern oak tree is, in a sense, unnatural. In its normal state it grows in woods beside other trees and has to compete for all the available light. This means that the trees would be tall, thin and straight with branches only at the top. Such oak trees make ideal timber for building purposes. Today we are used to seeing the spreading gnarled oak tree standing alone.

The right wood for the job

Iron Age farmers probably spent a lot of time in the woods searching out special shapes of timber that they could make into good tools. They might use a curving bough for a plow beam, a forked ash for a pitch fork, or a heavier forked tree as a simple upright post to support a building.

The purpose in seeking out the special natural shapes for specific tools lies in the natural strength of the wood. If the shape of the tool follows the natural shape, the way the grain runs will allow the tool to stand up to greater strain without breaking. In addition to special shapes the farmers would be looking for convenient standard lengths of timber to make into fence posts, beams, planks, rafters and all kinds of household objects. Many hours would have been spent in the woodland selecting and cutting down trees, marking others for the following year, carting the timber back to the farmstead and stacking it carefully to allow the free circulation of air around and under the stacks. It is important to keep such a stack just clear of the ground; otherwise the damp will penetrate and rot the wood. Perhaps some of the pairs of post-holes so common in excavations represent the retaining timber uprights for woodstacks.

right: *A hazel tree left to grow wild. The timber from such a tree is unsuitable for building.*

far right: *Here all the old timber has been cut away and the stool carefully cleaned. The axe is a reconstruction of an Iron Age type.*

Wood for fuel

We can be quite sure that each farmstead possessed a large woodpile for burning on the hearths and in the ovens. It is quite possible that one fire was kept burning all the year round in every farmstead and for this a regular supply of wood would be needed. With such a permanent fire, the problems of fire-lighting would be lessened. On the other hand it is not difficult to make a fire using the simple bow drill and dry leaves and twigs. Flint also could have been used to strike sparks.

Another winter task that was necessary for all-year-round supplies was the making of charcoal for the ovens. We have seen that because the narrow opening to the oven limits the amount of oxygen, charcoal must be used instead of wood. Making charcoal is a skill that has survived for thousands of years. Charcoal is even now manufactured on the same principles though in modern kilns. The old-fashioned process is exactly the same as firing pottery in a pit clamp, except that the clamp is much bigger and contains only wood.

Once the short cold days of winter begin to lengthen, and spring returns, the whole cycle of farming begins over again.

The first-year growth, after cutting, shows the new hazel rods. In seven years these will be ideal for hurdle and wattle work.

48

Index

looms, 45-46
lynchets, 8

manure used as fertilizer, 11, 12, 19, 39
melde ('fat hen'), 11, 31, 40
metalwork, 36

ovens, 29
oxen. *See* cattle

pannage, 16-17
peat bogs, Danish, evidence found in,
   6, 10-11, 45
pigs, 16-17
pit clamp, 34-35
pits: as archaeological evidence, 21,
   28; use of, 21, 31, 41-43
plowing: equipment for, 6-7; size of
   fields for, 8; use of pigs for, 16-17
post-holes as archaeological evidence,
   16, 21, 22, 24, 28-29, 45, 47
pottery: as evidence, 10, 11, 32; making
   of, 33-36; storage of clay for, 43; use
   of, 43

reaping, 37-38
reconstruction, of Iron Age life
   conditions, 4, 22, 27, 28-29
Romans. *See* classical writers,
   comments of, on Iron Age in Britain
roof, construction of, 24-26
roundhouses, construction of: of stone,
   22-24; of wood, 24-27

salt, 31
seeds: sowing of, 9; storage of, 41-43;
   types of, 10-11
sheep, Soay, 12-13
silage, 21
sowing, 9
spelt wheat, 11, 37, 39
spinning of wool, 45
straw: preparation of, 38; use of, for
   thatching, 22, 26; use of, in kilns, 34

thatching, 22, 25-26
tools: for building, 24, 26; for farming,
   19, 38, 47, 48; for household use, 32,
   36, 45
trade: of grain, 41, 43; of salt, 31
turf: for firing pottery, 34; for walls, 27

utensils. *See* tools

vetch, 11, 21, 40

weaving, 45-46
weeding, 11
wheat, 11, 37, 39
willow withes, 22, 24
wood: for building, 22, 24-25, 47; care
   of trees for, 47; for fires, 48; for tools,
   21, 36, 47
wool: plucking of sheep for, 12-13;
   spinning of, 45; weaving of, 45-46

yealms, 26, 38
yokes, 7

Acknowledgments

The author and publisher wish to thank the following for permission to reproduce illustrations:
p.6 after H. O. Hansen in *Tools and Tillage*, 1 (2), 1969; pp.8, 15 University of Cambridge Committee for Aerial Photography; p.10 (Bog man) Forhistorish Museum, Moesgård, Denmark; p.10 (seed impressions) National Museum of Antiquities, Scotland; p.14 Peter Baker; p.15 (coin) City Museum, Bristol; p.16 (Gundestrup cauldron) Danish National Museum; p.18 (dog skeleton) Dorset County Museum; p.25 (ring beam) Waldo S. Lanchester; p.28 *Proceedings of the Prehistoric Society*, NS, VI (1), 1940; p.36 (torc) The Trustees of the British Museum; p.36 (ladle), 47 (tools) Glastonbury Antiquarian Society; pp.39, 40 drawings by Sybil J. Roles from Clapham, Tutin and Warburg, *Flora of the British Isles*, published by C.U.P. 1965; p.42 *Proceedings of the Prehistoric Society*, 40, 1974; p.45 University of Cambridge Museum of Archaeology and Anthropology, photograph Abbas Hashemi.
All other photographs are the author's.

Cover and text illustrations by Valerie Bell

The Cambridge History Library

The Cambridge Introduction to History
Written by Trevor Cairns

PEOPLE BECOME CIVILIZED

THE ROMANS AND THEIR EMPIRE

BARBARIANS, CHRISTIANS, AND MUSLIMS

THE MIDDLE AGES

EUROPE AROUND THE WORLD

EUROPE AND THE WORLD

THE BIRTH OF MODERN EUROPE

THE OLD REGIME AND THE REVOLUTION

POWER FOR THE PEOPLE

The Cambridge Topic Books
General Editor Trevor Cairns

THE AMERICAN WAR OF INDEPENDENCE

BENIN: AN AFRICAN KINDGOM AND CULTURE

THE BUDDHA

BUILDING THE MEDIEVAL CATHEDRALS

CHRISTOPHER WREN
AND ST. PAUL'S CATHEDRAL

THE EARLIEST FARMERS AND THE FIRST CITIES

EARLY CHINA AND THE WALL

THE FIRST SHIPS AROUND THE WORLD

GANDHI AND THE STRUGGLE
FOR INDIA'S INDEPENDENCE

HERNAN CORTES: CONQUISTADOR IN MEXICO

THE INDUSTRIAL REVOLUTION BEGINS

LIFE IN A FIFTEENTH-CENTURY MONASTERY

LIFE IN A MEDIEVAL VILLAGE

LIFE IN THE IRON AGE

LIFE IN THE OLD STONE AGE

MARTIN LUTHER

MEIJI JAPAN

THE MURDER OF ARCHBISHOP THOMAS

MUSLIM SPAIN

THE NAVY THAT BEAT NAPOLEON

POMPEII

THE PYRAMIDS

THE ROMAN ARMY

THE ROMAN ENGINEERS

ST. PATRICK AND IRISH CHRISTIANITY

THE VIKING SHIPS

The Cambridge History Library will be expanded in the future to include additional volumes. Lerner Publications Company is pleased to participate in making this excellent series of books available to a wide audience of readers.

Lerner Publications Company
241 First Avenue North, Minneapolis, Minnesota 55401